Of Mice ar
Classroom C

A SCENE BY SCENE TEACHING GUIDE

Amy Farrell

SCENE BY SCENE

ENNISKERRY, IRELAND

Scene by Scene
Enniskerry
Wicklow, Ireland.
www.scenebysceneguides.com

Of Mice and Men Classroom Questions by Amy Farrell. —1st ed.
ISBN 978-1-910949-51-1

Contents

Chapter 1

Summary

Lennie and George are in the beautiful Soledad countryside.

They are opposites; George is small and sharp, while Lennie is large and slow-witted.

George is annoyed that the bus driver let them off where he did, forcing them to walk for miles in the heat.

Lennie does not know where they are headed, he has forgotten. He says he remembers about the rabbits though, to George's annoyance.

George has work cards for both of them, he has arranged work on a ranch.

Lennie pets a dead mouse until George takes it from him.

George is in charge and reminds Lennie that they do not want any trouble like they had in Weed.

George talks about all he could do if it were not for Lennie, but feels bad when Lennie asks him if he should leave.

George tells Lennie that they are not like other guys and tells Lennie how good it will be when they get their own place.

George tells Lennie to return to this spot in the brush if he gets in trouble.

Points to Consider

Steinbeck makes great use of description to set the scene and show the peace and tranquility of nature. This pool-side location is significant, as it will be re-visited at the novel's close.

The relationship between the men is quickly established, with Lennie's dependence on George clearly evident. It can be interesting to discuss the men's characters and see how students assess their personalities and the relationship between them.

The reference to trouble in Weed is important, as it foreshadows the trouble that is to come for the men.

Lennie's petting of the dead mouse is significant, for it not only highlights his simple, child-like character, but prepares us for what happens later on with the puppy, and Curley's wife.

George's comments about how easy life would be without Lennie are worth discussing, as this situation will arise at the novel's close. Generally, students tend to disbelieve George when he says that leaving Lennie would make him happy.

Questions

1.   Describe the setting as this novel begins.

2.   Describe the men who arrive at the pool.
        Give as much detail as you can in your answer.

3.   What does Lennie have in his pocket?
        What is your reaction to this?
        Does this tell you anything about him?

4.   How will the men get work?

5.   What happened in Weed?

6.   Does Lennie make life difficult for George?
        Why does George stay with Lennie?

7.   Lennie and George think they are not like the other men
        working on ranches.
        Why is this the case?

8.   What 'dream' are the men working towards?
        Does this sound appealing to you?
        Give reasons for your answer.

9.   If Lennie gets into trouble, what must he do?
        Does this sound like a good plan to you?

10.   Describe the relationship between these two men, as you
        see it. Refer to the positives and negatives of their
        friendship.

Chapter 2

Summary

An old man (Candy) shows George and Lennie to their bunks. He tells them that the boss is annoyed that they did not arrive the night before.

George blames their lateness on the bus driver. He does all the talking with the boss, speaking for Lennie as well as himself. This makes the boss suspicious of George; he thinks George may be taking Lennie's money from him. George responds by saying that Lennie is his cousin.

When the boss leaves, George blames Lennie for the boss's questions and tells him again to keep his mouth shut.

Curley, the boss's son, comes in looking for his father. He tries to talk to Lennie and gets annoyed when George cuts in on his behalf. When he leaves, the old man tells them that Curley likes to pick fights with big guys. George feels that Lennie would be well able to handle Curley.

The old swamper says that Curley has been worse since he got married. He says that Curley's wife has been giving other men the eye.

George is worried about Curley and he warns Lennie to keep away from him.

Curley's wife comes to the bunkhouse, looking for Curley. George thinks she is a tramp, but Lennie is struck by how pretty she is. George warns him to keep away from her.

Lennie does not want to stay at the ranch, but George tells him that they have to stick with it long enough to get a stake together.

Slim and Carlson come in from bucking barley. Carlson suggests shooting the old swamper's (Candy's) dog and replacing it with a pup from Slim's bitch's litter.

Lennie is excited at the prospect of a pup, wanting George to ask for one for him right away.

The two men are leaving to go to dinner when Curley comes in looking for his wife.

Points to Consider

It may be necessary to prepare students for the racist terms used in this chapter. They may be shocked at the use of the term "nigger".

When George tries to speak on Lennie's behalf, the boss assumes that George is trying to make some money out of his companion. This is interesting, as it adds to the themes of friendship and isolation in the novel.

It can be rewarding to discuss the world of the novel, the kind of place that it is, to help students imagine both the setting and the atmosphere of the time.

At this early stage of the story it is interesting to discuss the relationships between characters, and whether they are positive or negative. This will help students develop a feel for the atmosphere and storyline.

Students' reactions to Slim's drowning of four of the puppies and Carlson's comments about Candy's dog, add to their understanding of the world of the novel. They may find it is a lonely, harsh, unfeeling place, characterised by cruelty and a lack of human warmth, despite the large number of characters living together.

Questions

1. Describe the bunkhouse.

2. What complaint does George have about their bunks?

3. How does the boss react to Lennie and George arriving later than expected?
   What is your reaction to this?

4. According to the old man, how did the men on the ranch celebrate Christmas?
   What is your response to this?

5. What makes the boss suspicious of the new arrivals?

6. "If I was a relative of yours I'd shoot myself."
   Is George mean to Lennie?

7. Assess the character of Curley, the boss's son, based on how he acts and what the old man (Candy) says about him.

8. Is George intimidated by Curley?
   What makes you say this?

9. How does the old man (Candy) speak about Curley's wife?
   What is your reaction to this?

10. George tells Lennie that he is scared.
    Why does he feel this way?

11.   Briefly describe Curley's wife.

           Are the men's comments about her entirely fair?

           What do their comments reveal about this world?

12.   Briefly describe Slim.

           Does he sound like a typical ranch worker?

           Explain your point of view.

13.   Why is Carlson interested in Slim's pups?

           What is your reaction to this idea?

14.   Would you like to work on this ranch, from what you have read about life here? Give reasons for your answer.

15.   What, do you think, will happen next?

Chapter 3

Summary

George thanks Slim for giving one of his pups to Lennie. Slim is impressed that Lennie is so strong and is such a good worker. Slim is surprised that the men travel together, so George explains that they have been together for a long time.

George says that he used to make fun of Lennie in the past, but does not anymore. George goes on to tell Slim about the trouble they got into in Weed, when Lennie touched a girl's red dress and frightened her. The girl screamed when he touched her dress, and Lennie held on to her, not knowing what to do. When George got Lennie off her, she told the law she was raped. This is why the men left Weed in a hurry.

Lennie comes in, hiding his pup, but George makes him return it to the barn.

Candy and Carlson come in and Carlson complains about the smell of Candy's old dog. Carlson tells Candy he should really shoot the dog, but Candy does not want to, saying he has had the dog for a long time.

Carlson perseveres, and Candy gives in, telling Carlson he can shoot the animal. Carlson takes the dog out and the men listen for the gunshot. When it comes, Candy rolls over to face the wall.

Whit tells George that Curley's wife gives everybody the eye, that she can't keep away from guys.

He tells George about a brothel in town they go to on Saturday nights. George says he is saving his money for a stake with Lennie.

Curley comes in looking for his wife. He heads to the barn when he hears that is where Slim is, thinking that she is with Slim.

Lennie asks George to tell him about the place they are going to get together, and he does so, describing the dwellings, animals and crops they will have there.

Candy has been listening to their conversation. He offers the men three hundred and fifty dollars if they will let him join them. Candy is worried that he will be sacked from the ranch soon, due to his missing hand, so is keen to join the men.

George says they will do it together, excited at the prospect. He says that they will go in a month.

George tells Candy and Lennie not to tell anybody about their plan.

Candy says that he should have shot his dog himself, that he should not have let a stranger do it.

The other men return to the bunkhouse and Curley picks on Lennie, accusing him of laughing at him. Lennie tries to retreat, but Curley attacks him. Lennie does not defend himself, but calls to George to make Curley stop as Curley beats him.

George tells Lennie to get Curley, and so he grabs Curley's fist in one hand, squeezing it. When he does not let go, George slaps Lennie's face and shouts at him to release Curley, which he finally does.

Curley's hand is crushed. Slim arranges to take him to the doctor in Soledad. Slim tells Curley he better say his hand got caught in a machine. He threatens that if Lennie gets canned, they will make a laughing stock of Curley.

When Curley leaves, George reassures Lennie that it was not his fault. Lennie is worried that he will not get to tend the rabbits, but George tells him that he has done nothing wrong.

Points to Consider

We are provided with backstory surrounding George and Lennie's friendship. It is clear that despite his earlier grousing and complaining, George thinks very highly of Lennie.

George's account of the trouble Lennie got into in Weed is significant, as it foreshadows what is to come with Curley's wife. It is worth discussing Lennie's intellectual capabilities and how others must perceive him because of his strength and size.

The transient nature of the ranch workers and Candy's dog being shot, draws attention to the loneliness and isolation of ranch life in this chapter.

It may be worthwhile to discuss students' views of Curley's wife. Some may feel she is the two dimensional 'tramp' character that the men view her as, others will feel she is isolated and lonely.

George and Lennie's dream to get a stake together and live off the land is important. It sets them apart from the other men as they have a shared goal to work towards. Also, this place will be their own, not just somewhere where they are paid to work. It is unsurprising that this dream home is so appealing to those who hear of it.

Candy's remorse over not shooting his dog himself is important, as it foreshadows George's grim task in the closing chapter. It can be interesting to discuss whether students feel Candy should have shouldered this responsibility himself.

Lennie's reaction to being attacked by Curley shows that he is slow to anger or defend himself. However, the damage he does to Curley is considerable, it is worthwhile discussing whether he poses a danger on the ranch.

Questions

1. How does George feel about Lennie at the start of the chapter?

2. Slim remarks that ranch workers rarely travel together. What insight does this give you into the lives of the ranch workers?

3. How does George explain his friendship with Lennie to Slim?

4. George says he used to make fun of Lennie.
    Why did he stop?
    What does this tell you about George?

5. What happened in Weed that made Lennie and George run away?
    How does learning of this incident impact on the mood and atmosphere of the novel?

6. Why does Slim say that Lennie is like a kid?
    Do you agree with him?
    Explain your point of view with reference to the story.

7. Carlson is very keen for Candy to shoot his old dog.
    What are your views on this?

8. Does Candy want his dog to be shot?
    Why does he allow it?

9.   What does Whit say about Curley's wife?
     In general, do the men have a good opinion of her?
     What is your response to this?

10. Is George really serious about getting a stake with Lennie?
     Give reasons for your answer.

11. Why does Lennie ask George to tell him about their
     dream place?
     Does Lennie want this more than George does?

12. Describe the place they intend to get together.
     Does it sound appealing to you?
     What makes it appeal to the men so much?

13. Why does Lennie grumble and threaten their 'future' cats?
     What does this reveal to you about him?

14. What makes Candy want to join George and Lennie in
     their dream place?

15. Do you feel sorry for Candy in this chapter?
     Explain your reasons.

16. Describe Curley's mood when he returns to the
     bunkhouse.
     Why does he feel this way?

17. What makes Lennie fight back when Curley attacks him?
     Does he intend to hurt Curley?
     Do you condemn or condone Lennie's actions here?

18. Describe the fight between Curley and Lennie.
    What injuries do they sustain?

19. What is stopping Curley from getting Lennie in trouble
    because of the fight?

20. Is George annoyed with Lennie for fighting with Curley?

21. Do you think Lennie's fight with Curley could lead to
    problems later on? Explain your point of view.

22. Is George a good friend to Lennie?
    Use examples from the story to support your point of
    view.

Chapter 4

Summary

This chapter begins in Crooks' quarters. He is a crippled, black, stable hand. He bunks in the harness room, separate to the other men.

Crooks is rubbing liniment onto his back when Lennie appears in his doorway. Crooks tells him off for coming into his room uninvited, but he begins to talk to him all the same.

Crooks is isolated from the other men because he is black.

Lennie tells Crooks about the rabbits and their plan to live off the fat of the land.

Crooks talks to Lennie and says George has got it right, having someone to talk to.

Crooks worries Lennie by suggesting that George might not come back from town, that he might get hurt or killed. Lennie demands to know who hurt George, so Crooks backs down and says that George is fine and will be back again.

Crooks talks about the way he cannot go into the bunkhouse because of his skin colour, how he has to sit alone and read or think.

Crooks dismisses Lennie's talk of a place of their own, saying that it is what all men on ranches dream of.

Candy comes into the barn, looking for Lennie. At first Crooks says they won't ever get a place of their own, but he is convinced by Candy. Crooks offers to join them and work for his board.

Curley's wife appears, looking for Curley. She says that she likes to talk to people and complains about listening to Curley. She asks what happened to Curley's hand, but Candy will not tell her. This makes her angry and she insults the men. Candy stands up to her, saying that she is not wanted there and that it does not matter if she gets them canned because soon they will have their own place.

Curley's wife sees the bruises on Lennie's face and figures out how Curley got injured. Crooks tries to throw her out and she threatens him. Candy says he and Lennie will back Crooks up if she says anything, but she replies that nobody would believe them.

Candy says he heard the guys returning and that she better go.

She tells Lennie that she is glad he hurt Curley a bit and leaves.

Crooks is keen for Candy and Lennie to leave. George comes looking for Lennie. Crooks tells Candy that he has changed his mind about working for them when they get a place. The men leave.

Points to Consider

Crooks, the black stable buck, is quite brusque with Lennie when he first meets him. It can be worthwhile to hear students' opinions about why he treats Lennie this way.

Crooks, like Candy, is an outsider, who does not fully fit in with the other men. This contributes to the idea that theirs is a cold, unfeeling world, with little compassion or friendship. His conversation with Lennie reveals the depth of his loneliness and isolation.

Crooks and Candy have physical disabilities, something that hinders them severely in this physical, masculine world of the ranch.

Crooks wants to join the men in their 'dream place' when he hears Candy talking about it. It is worth discussing why these men find this idea so attractive.

Candy, like Lennie, views George as a leader, someone to look up to. His reasons for seeing him this way can be interesting to discuss.

The racism of their world is obvious in this chapter. Crooks lives a lonely, isolated life and is looked down on by the other men. Curley's wife's threats towards the end of the chapter remind us of his position in their society.

Questions

1. What does Crooks' room tell you about him?

2. Is Crooks happy to see Lennie when he appears in his room?

3. Does Crooks play cards with the other men?
   Why/ why not?
   What is your response to this?

4. Is Crooks a lonely character? Explain your view.

5. Why does Lennie get worried about George?
   Should Crooks have said this to Lennie?
   What made him say this to Lennie, in your opinion?

6. At first, does Crooks believe that Lennie and George will achieve their dream of having land of their own?

7. How does Crooks react to Candy coming into his room?
   Can you explain how he is feeling here?

8. What makes Crooks want to work with Lennie and George on their dream place?

9. Curley's wife calls Lennie, Candy and Crooks weak.
   Why does she insult them this way?

10. Why don't the men want to talk to Curley's wife?

    Is she a lonely character?

    Are there many lonely characters in this novel?

    Explain your point of view.

11. Do Curley and his wife get on well together?

    Do they have a strong relationship?

    Use examples from the text to support your viewpoint.

12. Candy is not afraid of annoying Curley's wife.

    Why is this the case?

13. How does Curley's wife threaten Crooks?

    What is your response to this?

14. Assess Curley's wife's character, using examples to support the points that you make.

15. What makes Crooks decide against joining the others in their dream place?

    How does this make you feel?

16. Assess Crooks' character, using examples to support the points that you make.

17. Is the ranch a nice place to live, from Crooks' perspective?

18. What does this chapter reveal to you about racism in the world of the novel?

    Include examples in your answer.

Chapter 5

Summary

Lennie is in the barn, looking at his dead puppy. He has killed it, accidentally. Lennie talks to the pup, afraid that he will get in trouble with George for killing it. He gets angry with the pup and throws it down, saying that now he will not get to tend the rabbits.

Curley's wife comes into the barn and Lennie hides the pup. He tells her that he is not allowed to talk to her, but this does not deter her. She says she never gets to talk to anyone and is awfully lonely.

Lennie tells her about the pup and she sympathises. He is still reluctant to talk to her though, as George warned him not to.

Curley's wife is annoyed by this. She talks about her past, saying she could have been an actress. She says that she does not like Curley.

She asks Lennie why he likes rabbits so much and he explains that he likes to pet soft things. She invites him to feel her hair, because it is soft and fine, so he does.

She tells him to stop, that he will mess it up, and jerks her head sideways.

Lennie panics and hangs on to her hair. She starts to scream and Lennie covers her mouth with his hand to stop her. He gets annoyed that she is yelling, afraid that he will get in trouble, and shakes her, accidentally breaking her neck.

Lennie realises he has done a bad thing when she does not move. He takes off for the brush, taking the dead pup with him to throw away.

Candy comes into the barn, looking for Lennie, and discovers Curley's wife. He goes to get George.

George says they better tell the others, but Candy is afraid that Curley will lynch Lennie. To Candy's disappointment, George realises that they will never get a little place of their own now.

George asks Candy to 'discover' the body in a few minutes, when he is in the bunkhouse, so the other men will not think that he knew anything about it.

Candy is angry, blaming Curley's wife for ruining their dream plan.

The men come in and Slim checks for a pulse. Curley immediately says Lennie is the culprit. He goes for his shotgun, planning to shoot Lennie in the guts.

Slim says they better go after Lennie. He knows that Curley wants to shoot him, but thinks that locking him in a cage would be no good either.

Carlson's gun is missing. He thinks that Lennie has taken it.

Curley wants George to go with them. He agrees, but asks Curley not to shoot Lennie. Curley says that of course they will shoot him, that he has

Carlson's Luger.

Slim suggests that Curley should stay with his wife, but Curley plans to catch Lennie and shoot his guts out.

Candy stays with the dead girl and George leaves with the men.

Points to Consider

This chapter opens with Lennie in the barn with the pup he has accidentally killed. Some students will not be surprised that he has killed the pup, as there have been hints up to this point that he does not realise his own strength.

Lennie is upset about what he has done and does not want to get into trouble with George. His concern here will give students an insight into his thinking process and what George means to him.

Curley's wife's loneliness and isolation are clear in her conversation with Lennie. She is a desperately lonely character in search of companionship.

Lennie's accidental killing of Curley's wife is not entirely unexpected, it is foreshadowed by the pup's death in the very same location. As the most exciting and dramatic event up to this point, it is worth discussing students' reactions to it. Some will have seen it coming, some will feel Lennie is not entirely to blame, some will be shocked by this violent turn, etc.

When George first sees Curley's wife's body, he realises straight away what Lennie has done. It is interesting to discuss whether there is a sense of the inevitable here, whether the men's dream was doomed to fail, or whether they could have achieved their goal.

Curley's plan to shoot Lennie in the guts shows his cruelty and viciousness. The men's willingness to chase Lennie down shows the brutality of their world. George does little to stop them, showing his acceptance of Lennie's fate.

Questions

1. What has happened to Lennie's pup?
   Should we have expected this to happen?
   Explain your point of view.

2. Why is Lennie angry with the pup?
   Does this reaction tell you anything about Lennie?

3. Why does Curley's wife talk to Lennie?

4. According to Lennie, what happened to his pup?
   What is your response to this?

5. Why doesn't Lennie want to talk to Curley's wife?

6. Does Curley's wife sound happy and content with her life?

7. Why does Lennie like rabbits?
   Does this tell you anything about him?

8. Why does Lennie touch Curley's wife?
   Why does he hurt her?

9. What is your reaction to this incident in the barn?
   Are you shocked by it?

10. Does Lennie intend to kill Curley's wife?
    Is Lennie responsible for her death?

11. When he sees Curley's wife's body, what does George
    decide to do?

12.   What course of action does Candy think is best?

13.   Is their dream of living off the fat of the land still possible?

14.   Does George view Lennie differently because of what he has done?

15.   Is Candy upset about Curley's wife, Lennie or himself? Do you feel sorry for him?

16.   Describe the men's reactions when they discover the body. Are you surprised by Curley's reaction?

17.   Is this an exciting or sad section of the story? Explain what makes you feel as you do at this point.

18.   "Shoot for his guts." Comment on Curley's plan here. Does he seem upset by his wife's death, in your opinion?

19.   We never learn Curley's wife's name. What point is the author making here?

20.   How do you expect this story to end?

Chapter 6

Summary

It is peaceful and calm by the pool in the brush when Lennie appears.

He is worried that George will not want him anymore.

He imagines a little, old, fat woman, who tells him off for not listening to George and for doing bad things.

Next he imagines a giant rabbit. It tells him that he would never be able to tend rabbits and says that George is going to beat the hell out of him with a stick. Lennie is annoyed by this and tells the rabbit that George is nice to him and will not be mean. The rabbit upsets Lennie, telling him that George is going to leave him.

At this point George arrives and asks Lennie why he is yelling. Lennie asks George if he is going to leave him and George says that he will not. Lennie tells George that he has done another bad thing. He is surprised when George does not give him hell about this. George then says the usual things to give him hell, but without feeling.

Lennie says he can go off by himself, but George says that he wants him with him. Lennie asks George to tell him how they are different to other guys, because they have each other.

George tells Lennie to take off his hat and look across the river. He tells Lennie about the place they will get together, how they will live off the fat of the land. He tells Lennie that he has never been mad at him and that he is not mad now.

Voices come closer in the brush. George tells Lennie they will get their place right now and then shoots him in the back of the head.

George throws the gun away and Slim and the men arrive. Slim tells George that he had to do it and takes him to have a drink.

Curley and Carlson wonder what is the matter with George and Slim.

Points to Consider

The pool-side setting is significant here as it is where our story began. Also, the peace and quiet of the natural world seems at odds with the violent world of the men.

Lennie's concerns over upsetting George are quite touching here. He has no regard for himself, he focuses all his attention on his friend. This also shows his lack of understanding about what he has done.

Lennie's imaginings show his worries over upsetting George, but also the faith and belief he has in George, who has treated him so well. This insight and self-criticism on Lennie's part adds to the sadness of this section.

George's killing of his best friend is worth discussing in class. Some will wish the men ran away together, others will feel George had no choice, considering what Lennie had done.

It can be worthwhile to discuss what life will be like for George without Lennie. Imagining George's future helps students understand what Steinbeck suggests about life in this story.

Questions

1. Describe the setting as this chapter begins.
   What is the mood like?

2. How is Lennie feeling as he waits in the brush?

3. What different things does Lennie imagine?
   What do each of these reveal to you about Lennie?

4. Is Lennie aware that he has killed Curley's wife?
   Use examples to support your point of view.

5. Does Lennie expect George to punish him?
   What does this tell you about their friendship?

6. Is George angry with Lennie when he joins him?

7. George lies to Lennie, telling him that they will get their place together soon.
   Why does he lie to his best friend like this?

8. How does George telling the story of their dream impact on the mood here?

9. How do you feel at this point? Explain your response here.

10. What is your reaction to George's shooting of Lennie?

11. What makes him take his friend's life?
    How does this make you feel?

12. Slim tells George that he had to do this to Lennie.
    Do you agree with Slim?
    Does George have a choice here?
    If so, what other options does George have?

13. Carlson does not understand why George and Slim are upset.
    What does this tell you about Carlson and this world?

14. Does Lennie deserve to die for his crime?

15. What will life be like for George, without Lennie?

16. Are you saddened by the story's ending?
    Explain your response.

Further Questions

1. Is 'Of Mice and Men' a novel about society, isolation, friendship, or something else?
    Explain your point of view using examples from the novel.

2. Was George a true friend to Lennie?
    Should he have done more to protect him or prevent his crime?

3. Although they look for one another, the only time we see Curley and his wife together is when she is dead.
    What is the author telling us about their relationship?

4. This story is peopled with cruel, cold characters, in beautiful surroundings.
    What is the effect of this on the story?

5. Were Lennie and George doomed to fail?
    Could their dream ever be realised in the world of this novel?

6. Do hopes and dreams help or hinder the characters in this novel?

7. Are you surprised by the final scene or did you anticipate the ending?
   Explain your point of view.

8. How does Steinbeck make use of foreshadowing in this novel? What is the effect of this?

9. What do you like about this novel?
   Give examples in your answer.

10. What do you dislike about this novel?
    Give examples in your answer.

11. Who is your favourite character?
    What do you like or admire about them?

12. Which character do you dislike most?
    Explain what makes you dislike them.

13. What different elements of the story combine to make this novel exciting?

14. Do you like the ending?
    Does the ending complete the story?

15. Was there anything in the story that you would have liked to know more about?
    Explain your answer, using examples.

16. Would this story make a good movie?
    What actors would you choose to play the lead roles?
    Explain your choices.

17. Would you like to work on a ranch like the one in this novel? Why/why not?

18. Does this novel teach you anything about the time or place it is set in?

19. Do the characters in this story have good relationships with each other? Include examples in your answer.

20. What does this story teach us about loneliness?

21. What was your favourite section of the story? Why did this part appeal to you?

22. What was the saddest section of the story? What made it sad or moving?

23. Does this novel remind you of any other novels or films? Explain your view.

24. Would you recommend this novel to a friend? Why/why not?

CLASSROOM QUESTIONS GUIDES

Books of questions, designed to save teachers time and lead to rewarding classroom experiences.

SCENEBY
SCENE

www.SceneBySceneGuides.com

Lightning Source UK Ltd.
Milton Keynes UK
UKHW021933060819
347506UK00006B/177/P